GUARDIAN PROTECTION HOME SECURITY SYSTEM USER GUIDE

Set up, Installation, Troubleshooting and Maintenance, Everything You Need to Know about the Guardian Protection Smart Home Security

By

Celina Walter

1

Contents

1.

Overview of the Guardian Protection Home Security System

As someone who's always been passionate about keeping my home and loved ones safe, I was thrilled when I discovered the Guardian Protection home security system. This comprehensive system has quickly become an integral part of my daily life, providing me with peace of mind and a sense of security that I never thought possible.

Guardian Protection offers a full range of security features that cater to every need. From advanced sensors and cameras to a user-friendly control panel, every component is designed with the latest technology to ensure top-notch protection. Whether it's keeping an eye on things when I'm away or safeguarding my home while I sleep, Guardian Protection has it all covered.

One of the things that stood out to me was the system's versatility. It's not just a one-size-fits-all solution; it's customizable to fit my specific requirements. I was able to set up different security zones and adjust the sensitivity of the sensors, making the system work perfectly for my home. The mobile app has been excellent, allowing me to monitor everything remotely and receive real-time alerts on my phone.

What also impressed me was the professional monitoring service. Knowing that trained professionals are ready to respond to any emergency, day or night, adds an extra layer of security. It's like having a personal security team at my fingertips, ready to assist whenever needed.

In short, the Guardian Protection home security system is more than just a collection of gadgets; it's a comprehensive solution that combines technology, convenience, and peace of mind. Whether you're looking to protect your family, and your belongings, or simply have that extra sense of security, Guardian Protection has proven to be a reliable and indispensable part of my life.

About Guardian Protection

In the early days of the 1950s, nestled in the heart of Pittsburgh, Pennsylvania, a small yet ambitious company began its journey. Guardian Protection, originally founded as Guardian Alarm Systems, set out with a simple mission: to provide peace of mind to its customers through innovative security solutions.

Back then, home security was a luxury few could afford. The concept of a monitored alarm system was new and largely untested, but Guardian Alarm Systems was determined to change that. The founders, inspired by the post-war boom and the technological advancements of the time, saw an opportunity to bring reliable security to everyday Americans.

In the beginning, their services were basic- simple alarm systems that alerted homeowners and the local police to potential intrusions. These early systems, though rudimentary by today's standards, laid the groundwork for what would become a legacy of trust and innovation. Word of mouth quickly spread about the effectiveness of these alarm systems, and Guardian Alarm Systems began to grow.

As the decades rolled on, the company embraced the rapid advancements in technology. The 1970s saw the introduction of more sophisticated wired alarm systems, and by the 1980s, Guardian had established itself as a leader in the security industry. The company rebranded to Guardian Protection to reflect its expanded range of services, which now included fire alarms, environmental monitoring, and comprehensive security solutions for both homes and businesses.

The 1990s brought the digital revolution. Guardian Protection was quick to adopt these new technologies, pioneering the use of digital monitoring systems that provided real-time alerts and remote access capabilities. This period marked a significant shift towards more interactive and user-friendly security solutions, laying the foundation for the modern smart home systems we see today.

In the early 2000s, Guardian Protection once again led the industry by integrating wireless technology into their systems. This innovation allowed for easier installation and more flexible security options, making advanced home security accessible to a broader audience. The introduction of mobile apps further revolutionized how customers interacted with their security systems, offering unprecedented control and convenience.

Today, Guardian Protection stands as a testament to decades of relentless innovation and dedication to customer safety. Their modern home security systems are a blend of cutting-edge technology and user-centric design, featuring everything from smart home integration and professional monitoring to high-definition video surveillance and environmental sensors.

The company's journey from a small local alarm provider to a national leader in home security is a story of vision, resilience, and a commitment to excellence. Guardian Protection continues to evolve, always staying ahead of the curve to ensure that families and businesses across the country feel safe and secure.

Through the years, Guardian Protection has not only protected homes but has also built a community of trust and reliability. As they look to the future, their mission remains the same: to deliver peace of mind through innovative, dependable security solutions.

Importance of Home Security

When I think about the importance of home security, it goes beyond just protecting my property—it's about ensuring the safety and well-being of everyone in my household. A secure home is a foundation for a comfortable and stress-free life, where we can focus on what matters most without constantly worrying about potential threats.

Home security systems play a crucial role in deterring crime. The mere presence of visible security measures like cameras, alarms, and signs can make a significant difference in preventing break-ins and other crimes. Criminals are far less likely to target a home that appears well-protected, making these systems a powerful deterrent.

However, the value of home security extends beyond preventing theft. It also provides early warnings in emergencies, such as fires, gas leaks, or medical situations. Modern systems come equipped with sensors and alerts that can detect these dangers and notify both the homeowner and emergency services, potentially saving lives and reducing damage.

For me, home security isn't just about physical protection; it's also about peace of mind. Knowing that my home is being monitored gives me confidence, whether I'm at work, travelling, or simply sleeping at night. It's reassuring to know that I can check in on my home from anywhere using a mobile app and receive instant notifications if something is amiss.

Moreover, a well-secured home can also have practical benefits, such as potentially lowering insurance premiums. Many insurance providers offer discounts for homes equipped with security systems, recognizing the reduced risk of incidents.

In a world where we can't always control external factors, having a robust home security system is one way we can take charge of our safety. It provides a vital layer of protection for our families, our possessions, and our peace of mind, making it an essential investment in our overall well-being.

Features and Benefits of the Guardian Protection

When I first explored the Guardian Protection home security system, I was impressed by the array of features it offers. Each component is thoughtfully designed to provide comprehensive security coverage, tailored to meet various needs. Here's a breakdown of the key features and benefits that make this system stand out:

Key Features

1. **Advanced Sensors and Detectors**

   o **Door and Window Sensors:** These sensors alert me whenever a door or window is opened unexpectedly, providing an essential first line of defence.

   o **Motion Detectors:** Strategically placed motion detectors can identify unusual movement within the home, ensuring that any unauthorized presence is detected promptly.

   o **Glass Break Sensors:** These sensors are particularly useful for detecting any attempts to break into the house through windows.

2. **High-Resolution Cameras**

   o **Indoor and Outdoor Cameras:** The cameras offer clear, high-resolution footage, allowing me to monitor both the interior and exterior of my home in real time.

- o **Night Vision:** This feature ensures that the cameras capture clear images even in low-light conditions, offering 24/7 surveillance.

3. **User-Friendly Control Panel**

   - o The central hub of the system, the control panel, is intuitive and easy to navigate. It allows me to arm and disarm the system, customize settings, and manage all connected devices effortlessly.

4. **Mobile App Integration**

   - o The Guardian Protection mobile app is a game-changer, providing remote access to the system. I can check live camera feeds, receive alerts, and control all security settings from anywhere in the world.

5. **Professional Monitoring Services**

   - o For added peace of mind, the system offers professional monitoring services. This means that trained professionals are on standby to respond to alarms and emergencies, ensuring a swift response in critical situations.

SECURITY

Alarm Siren with Strobe Light

6. **Smart Home Integration**

   o The system integrates seamlessly with various smart home devices, allowing me to create a connected ecosystem. Whether it's controlling lights, locks, or thermostats, the integration enhances both security and convenience.

Benefits

1. **Enhanced Security and Deterrence**

   o The comprehensive coverage provided by the sensors and cameras acts as a strong deterrent to potential intruders. The mere presence of a security system can discourage criminal activity.

2. **Real-Time Alerts and Monitoring**

   o Being able to receive real-time alerts and monitor my home remotely gives me confidence, knowing I can respond quickly to any situation. This feature is invaluable when I'm away from home.

3. **Emergency Response**

   o In the event of an emergency, the system's professional monitoring service ensures that help is on the way. This rapid response can be crucial in situations like break-ins, fires, or medical emergencies.

4. **Customization and Flexibility**

   o The ability to customize the system to fit my specific needs is a major benefit. I can adjust sensor sensitivity, set up different security zones, and choose from various monitoring options.

5. **Convenience and Control**

   o The integration with smart home devices adds an extra layer of convenience. I can control everything from my smartphone, making it easy to manage the system and other connected devices.

6. **Peace of Mind**

   o Ultimately, the greatest benefit of the Guardian Protection system is the peace of mind it provides. Knowing that my home and loved ones are protected allows me to focus on enjoying life without constantly worrying about security.

These features make the Guardian Protection home security system an invaluable asset for anyone looking to enhance the safety and security of their home.

2.

Getting Started

When I first decided to set up the Guardian Protection home security system, I found the process straightforward and user-friendly. Here's a guide to help you get started and ensure that everything is in place for a smooth installation and setup experience.

Package Contents

Upon unboxing your Guardian Protection system, you'll find the following components:

- **Control Panel:** The central hub of the system, which manages all connected devices and sensors.

- **Door/Window Sensors:** These sensors detect when doors or windows are opened.

- **Motion Detectors:** These are used to sense movement within your home.

- **Cameras:** Indoor and outdoor cameras for video monitoring.

- **Glass Break Sensors:** Designed to detect the sound of breaking glass.

- **Key Fobs and Keypads:** These are for easy arming and disarming of the system.

SECURITY

Key Fob

- **Power Adapters and Cables:** Necessary for powering the control panel and other devices.

- **Mounting Hardware:** Screws, brackets, and adhesive strips for installing sensors and cameras.

- **Quick Start Guide:** A booklet providing basic setup instructions.

System Requirements

Before starting the installation, it's essential to ensure that you meet the system requirements:

- **Stable Internet Connection:** The system requires a reliable Wi-Fi network for proper operation, including live streaming from cameras and receiving alerts.

- **Smartphone or Tablet:** For setting up the system and managing it via the Guardian Protection mobile app.

- **Power Outlets:** Ensure you have accessible power outlets for all components that require power.

Unboxing and Initial Inspection

1. **Inspect the Components:** Carefully unpack each item and check for any visible damage. Ensure that all components listed in the package contents are present.

2. **Read the Quick Start Guide:** Before diving into the installation, take a few minutes to read through the Quick Start Guide. It provides essential information and tips for setting up your system.

3. **Choose Installation Locations:** Decide where to place each component. Consider the following for optimal performance:

   o **Control Panel:** Install in a central, easily accessible location.

   o **Door/Window Sensors:** Place on all entry points, including doors and windows on the ground floor.

   o **Motion Detectors:** Position in areas with high traffic or potential entry points, like hallways and living rooms.

   o **Cameras:** Install at strategic points both inside and outside the home to cover key areas.

   o **Glass Break Sensors:** Place near windows or glass doors that are vulnerable to breakage.

4. **Check for Compatibility:** If you have existing smart home devices, check compatibility with the Guardian Protection system to ensure seamless integration.

By following these steps, I found that the installation process was much smoother and more efficient. Proper preparation is key to a successful setup, ensuring that all components are correctly placed and functioning as intended.

3.

Installation and Setup

Setting up the Guardian Protection home security system was also simple with a little planning and following the steps provided in the Quick Start Guide. Below is a detailed guide to help you install and set up your system efficiently.

Choose the Right Location for Components

Before installation, it's essential to strategically choose the locations for all components to ensure optimal coverage and performance:

1. **Control Panel:** Place the control panel in a central, easily accessible area, away from windows and doors to prevent tampering. It should be at a comfortable height for easy access.

2. **Door/Window Sensors:** Install these sensors on all entry points, including main doors, side doors, and accessible windows. Position the sensor on the door/window frame and the magnet on the moving part, ensuring they align properly when closed.

3. **Motion Detectors:** Position motion detectors in areas that intruders are likely to pass through, such as hallways, living rooms, and near-staircases. Avoid placing them near heat sources or vents to prevent false alarms.

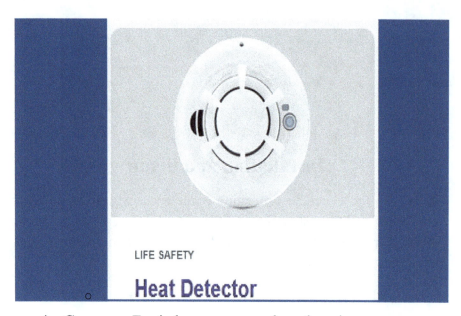

LIFE SAFETY

Heat Detector

4. **Cameras:** For indoor cameras, place them in common areas like living rooms or entrances. Outdoor cameras should cover entry points and vulnerable areas such as driveways and backyards. Make sure they are mounted at a sufficient height to avoid tampering and have a clear view.

SECURITY

Indoor Camera

5. **Glass Break Sensors:** Install these sensors in rooms with large windows or glass doors. Position them within 20 feet of the glass surface to effectively detect breakage sounds.

Installing the Control Panel

1. **Mount the Control Panel:** If the control panel is wall-mounted, use the provided mounting hardware to secure it. Ensure it's within reach of a power outlet and has a strong Wi-Fi signal.

2. **Power Up the Panel:** Connect the control panel to the power source using the provided adapter. The panel will start up and guide you through the initial setup process.

Setting Up Sensors

1. **Install Door/Window Sensors:** Clean the surface where you'll mount the sensors. Attach the sensor to the stationary part (frame) and the magnet to the moving part (door/window). Ensure the gap between them is minimal when closed.

2. **Position Motion Detectors:** Mount motion detectors at a height of about 6-7 feet for optimal coverage. Angle them towards the areas you want to monitor

3. **Mount Cameras:** Secure the cameras using the provided brackets and screws. Connect them to power and the network as needed. Adjust the angles to ensure they cover the desired areas.

4. **Install Glass Break Sensors:** Mount these sensors on walls or ceilings, within the recommended range of the glass surface they are monitoring.

Connecting to Power and Network

1. **Power Up All Devices:** Connect all devices to their respective power sources. Ensure that batteries are installed in wireless components where necessary.

SECURITY

Wireless Video Doorbell

2. **Connect to Wi-Fi:** Follow the on-screen instructions on the control panel to connect the system to your Wi-Fi network. This step is crucial for enabling remote access and notifications.

Downloading and Installing the Guardian Protection Mobile App

Open the App Store/Play Store:

- For iOS devices: Open the App Store.
- For Android devices: Open the Google Play Store.
- Search for Guardian Protection:
- In the search bar, type "Guardian Protection".
- Download the App:
- Find the Guardian Protection app in the search results.
- Tap "Download" or "Install".
- Open the App:
- Once the installation is complete, open the app from your home screen or app drawer.
- Sign In/Register:
- If you already have an account, enter your login details.
- If you don't have an account, follow the prompts to register.
- Set Up the App:
- Follow the on-screen instructions to complete the setup process.

- Customize your settings as needed to fit your security preferences.
- Explore Features:
- Familiarize yourself with the app's features, such as arm/disarm system, view security camera feeds, and receive notifications.

If you encounter any issues during the download or installation process, refer to the Guardian Protection website for troubleshooting tips or contact their customer support for assistance

Initial System Test and Troubleshooting

1. **System Test:** After installation, perform a complete system test to ensure all components are working correctly. Check each sensor and camera to confirm they are communicating with the control panel.

2. **Adjust Settings:** Fine-tune the settings, such as sensor sensitivity, camera angles, and notification preferences, to suit your needs.

3. **Troubleshooting:** If any components are not functioning as expected, refer to the troubleshooting section of the manual or contact customer support for assistance.

Note:

1. For easy identification, label each sensor and detector according to its location (e.g., "Front Door," "Living Room Motion").

2. Familiarize yourself with the user manual to understand all the features and functions of your system.

4.

System Configuration

After installing the Guardian Protection home security system, I found that configuring it to suit my specific needs was crucial too.

Navigating the Control Panel

The control panel is the heart of the system, where all the configuration and management take place. Here's how to get started:

1. **Initial Setup:** Upon powering up, the control panel will guide you through the initial setup, including language selection, time zone configuration, and connecting to Wi-Fi.

2. **Main Menu:** Access the main menu to explore various options like system status, device settings, and security modes. The interface is typically intuitive, with touch or button controls.

3. **Help and Support:** The control panel often includes a help section with tips and guidance, making it easy to troubleshoot or learn about features.

Customizing Settings

1. **Security Modes:** Configure different security modes such as "Home," "Away," and "Stay." Each mode can have unique settings for arming sensors and cameras. For instance, in

"Home" mode, motion sensors inside might be disabled while door/window sensors remain active.

2. **User Codes:** Set up multiple user codes for family members or trusted individuals. This allows for personalized access and helps track who disarms the system and when.

3. **Alarm Settings:** Adjust the alarm volume, duration, and types of alerts (audible, silent, or push notifications). Customize how you are alerted to different types of events.

4. **Notification Preferences:** Choose how to receive notifications (email, SMS, push notifications) and what events trigger alerts, such as motion detection, door openings, or system tampering.

5. **Sensor and Camera Settings:** Fine-tune the sensitivity of motion detectors, set up activity zones for cameras, and schedule when cameras should record or be on standby.

Integrating with Smart Home Devices

Guardian Protection offers compatibility with various smart home devices, enhancing both security and convenience:

1. **Smart Locks:** Integrate smart locks with your system to control door access remotely and check lock status. Some systems allow locking/unlocking doors automatically when arming or disarming the system.

AUTOMATION

Smart Door Lock

2. **Lighting Controls:** Connect smart lights to automate lighting, such as turning lights on when motion is detected or setting schedules for added security.

3. **Thermostats:** Integrate smart thermostats to manage home climate control, even when away, which can also help save energy.

4. **Voice Assistants:** Use voice commands through platforms like Amazon Alexa or Google Assistant to control your security system hands-free, such as arming/disarming the system or checking the status.

Setting Up Zones and Partitions

For larger homes or properties with multiple buildings, setting up zones and partitions can help manage security more effectively:

1. **Zones:** Divide your property into zones (e.g., front yard, backyard, basement). This allows you to monitor and control different areas separately.

2. **Partitions:** For multi-tenant properties or areas with different access needs, partitions enable independent arming and

disarming of separate sections. This is useful for guest houses, rental units, or home offices.

Configuring Emergency Contacts

1. **Add Contacts:** Enter emergency contacts into the system, such as family members, neighbours, or friends. These contacts can be notified in case of alarms or emergencies.

2. **Emergency Services:** Include details for local emergency services (police, fire department), ensuring that the monitoring centre has accurate information for dispatch in case of an emergency.

3. **Medical Alerts:** If applicable, set up medical alert features, including details about any medical conditions or necessary equipment for responders to be aware of.

By thoroughly configuring these settings, I was able to tailor the Guardian Protection system to perfectly fit my home and lifestyle.

5.

Using the System

After setting up, the next step is learning how to use it effectively. This involves understanding how to arm and disarm the system, managing alerts and notifications, utilizing the mobile app for remote access, and leveraging additional features for comprehensive security coverage.

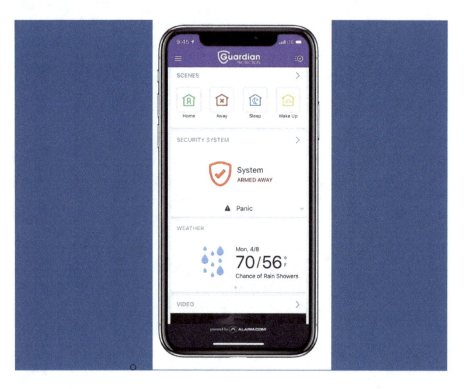

Arming and Disarming

The Guardian Protection system offers different modes to suit various situations:

1. **Home Mode:**

    o **Purpose:** This mode is ideal when you're at home and want to secure the perimeter while allowing free movement inside.

    o **How to Arm:** On the control panel or mobile app, select "Home" mode. Typically, this mode activates door and window sensors but disables indoor motion detectors.

2. **Away Mode:**

    o **Purpose:** Use this mode when the house is empty, as it provides maximum security by activating all sensors, including motion detectors.

    o **How to Arm:** Choose "Away" mode from the control panel or mobile app. Ensure all doors and windows are closed, as the system will monitor for any breaches.

3. **Stay Mode:**

    o **Purpose:** Similar to Home mode, but often used at night when you're at home and want extra security. It can be customized to your preferences.

    o **How to Arm:** Select "Stay" mode, which usually arms the perimeter sensors and specific indoor sensors, depending on your setup.

4. **Disarming the System:**

- o **How to Disarm:** Enter your user code on the control panel or use the mobile app. Disarming stops all active sensors and alerts.

Understanding Alerts and Notifications

The system can send various types of alerts to keep you informed:

1. **Intrusion Alerts:** Receive notifications if a door or window is opened unexpectedly, or if motion is detected when the system is armed.

2. **System Status Alerts:** Get updates on the system status, such as low battery warnings for sensors, connectivity issues, or system tampering.

3. **Environmental Alerts:** Some systems can monitor for environmental hazards like smoke, carbon monoxide, or flooding. Alerts will notify you if these sensors are triggered.

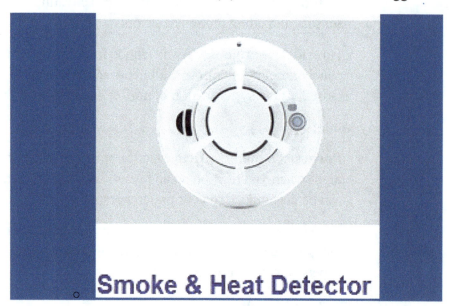

Smoke & Heat Detector

Using the Mobile App for Remote Access

The Guardian Protection mobile app is a powerful tool for managing your system on the go:

1. **Live Monitoring:** Access live feeds from your cameras, check the status of your sensors, and see a history of events.

2. **Remote Arming/Disarming:** Arm or disarm your system remotely, which is useful if you forget to set the alarm before leaving or need to let someone in while you're away.

3. **Smart Home Controls:** Control integrated smart devices, like lights or thermostats, directly from the app.

4. **Notifications and Alerts:** Customize your alert settings and receive push notifications for events like alarms, system status changes, or detected motion.

Monitoring Cameras and Recorded Footage

1. **Live View:** Use the app or control panel to view live footage from your cameras. This feature is especially useful for checking on your home while you're away.

2. **Recorded Footage:** Access recorded clips to review past events. This can be crucial for investigating incidents or simply keeping an eye on things.

3. **Two-Way Audio:** If your cameras support it, use two-way audio to communicate with anyone at your door or inside your home.

Panic and Emergency Features

1. **Panic Button:** The system often includes a panic button on the control panel or key fob. Pressing this button sends an

immediate alert to the monitoring centre, which can dispatch emergency services.

2. **Medical Alert:** For households with elderly members or individuals with medical conditions, the system can include features for medical alerts, quickly notifying the appropriate responders.

By mastering these features, I've found that I can effectively manage and use the system to ensure my home is secure. Whether at home or away, I have the peace of mind knowing that I can monitor and control my security system with ease.

6.

Maintenance and Troubleshooting

Regular maintenance and effective troubleshooting are crucial to ensuring the Guardian Protection home security system operates optimally. Here's a guide on how to keep the system in top condition and address common issues that might arise.

Regular Maintenance

1. **Battery Replacement:**

   o **Door/Window Sensors, Motion Detectors, and Key Fobs:** Most of these components are battery-operated. Check the battery status regularly and replace batteries as needed, typically every 6 to 12 months or as indicated by low battery alerts.

   o **Control Panel Backup Battery:** If the control panel has a backup battery, ensure it is in good condition to provide power during outages.

2. **Cleaning Sensors and Cameras:**

   o **Dust and Dirt:** Regularly clean sensors and camera lenses with a soft, dry cloth to prevent dust buildup, which can interfere with performance.

- Outdoor Cameras: Check for obstructions like spider webs or debris and clean the camera housing to maintain clear video quality.

3. **Software and Firmware Updates:**

    - **Control Panel and Mobile App:** Ensure the control panel and mobile app are updated to the latest software versions. This often includes security patches and new features.

    - **Camera Firmware:** Update the firmware of your cameras if new versions are released, enhancing performance and security.

4. **System Testing:**

    - **Regular Tests:** Periodically test all components of the system, including sensors, alarms, and cameras, to ensure they are functioning correctly. Many systems have a test mode that allows for safe testing without alerting the monitoring centre.

    - **Professional Inspections:** Consider scheduling annual inspections by a professional technician to assess the system's health and recommend any necessary upgrades or repairs.

Troubleshooting Common Issues

1. **Sensor Malfunctions:**

   o **Not Responding:** If a sensor is not responding, check the battery and replace it if necessary. Ensure the sensor is properly aligned and within range of the control panel.

   o **False Alarms:** Check for drafts, pets, or objects that could trigger motion detectors. Adjust the sensitivity settings if necessary.

2. **Camera Issues:**

   o **No Video Feed:** Ensure the camera is powered on and connected to the network. Check for any loose connections and reboot the camera if needed.

   o **Poor Image Quality:** Clean the camera lens and check for any network bandwidth issues that could affect video quality.

3. **Connectivity Problems:**

   o **Wi-Fi Connectivity:** If the control panel or cameras lose connection to Wi-Fi, check the router and network settings. Ensure the signal strength is adequate and consider repositioning the router or using a range extender.

   o **Mobile App Issues:** If the mobile app isn't working correctly, try restarting your phone, updating the app, or reinstalling it.

4. **Control Panel Issues:**

- o **Unresponsive Panel:** If the control panel is unresponsive, try rebooting it by unplugging it from the power source and plugging it back in. Check for any software updates that might need to be installed.

- o **Error Messages:** Refer to the user manual for specific error codes and troubleshooting steps. Often, these issues can be resolved by following the recommended actions.

5. **System Alerts and Notifications:**

- o **No Alerts:** If you're not receiving alerts, check the notification settings in the control panel and mobile app. Ensure that the correct contact information is entered and that notifications are enabled.

- o **False Alerts:** Review the settings for each sensor and adjust them if needed to prevent false alarms. This may include changing sensitivity levels or repositioning sensors.

Contacting Support and Professional Help

1. **Customer Support:** If you encounter issues that cannot be resolved through basic troubleshooting, contact Guardian Protection's customer support for assistance. They can provide guidance and may remotely diagnose problems.

2. **Professional Maintenance:** For complex issues or regular maintenance, consider hiring a professional technician to inspect and service your system.

With regular maintenance and knowing how to troubleshoot common problems, I've been able to keep my Guardian Protection system running smoothly.

7.

Security Best Practices

To get the most out of the Guardian Protection system, it's necessary to follow best practices that enhance overall security and ensure your system functions effectively. Here are some tips that I've found invaluable for maintaining a secure environment.

1. Regularly Update System Components

- **Firmware and Software Updates:** Always keep the control panel, cameras, and other smart devices up to date with the latest firmware and software updates. These updates often include critical security patches and new features.

- **Mobile App Updates:** Ensure that the Guardian Protection mobile app is always updated to the latest version to benefit from the newest security enhancements and features.

2. Secure Your Wi-Fi Network

- **Strong Passwords:** Use a strong, unique password for your Wi-Fi network. Avoid default settings and ensure your network name (SSID) doesn't reveal personal information.

- **Encryption:** Enable WPA3 encryption on your Wi-Fi router, or at least WPA2 if WPA3 is not available. This helps protect your data and prevents unauthorized access.

3. Use Strong, Unique Passwords

- **System Access:** Set strong, unique passwords for the control panel, mobile app, and any associated accounts. Avoid using easily guessable passwords like "1234" or "password."

- **User Codes:** For user codes, use different codes for each person with access, and avoid sharing these codes unnecessarily. Update these codes periodically.

4. Enable Two-Factor Authentication (2FA)

- **Account Security:** If available, enable two-factor authentication for your Guardian Protection account and any associated online services. This adds an extra layer of security by requiring a second form of verification, such as a text message or authentication app.

5. Regularly Test Your System

- **Routine Testing:** Regularly test all sensors, alarms, and cameras to ensure they are functioning correctly. Use the system's test mode to verify that each component is working as expected.

- **Simulate Scenarios:** Occasionally simulate scenarios like break-ins or emergencies to practice your response and ensure the system alerts function properly.

6. Limit Access to Your System

- **User Permissions:** Only grant system access to trusted individuals. Limit the number of users and ensure they understand how to use the system responsibly.

- **Guest Access:** If you need to provide temporary access (e.g., for house guests or service personnel), use temporary user codes that can be easily deactivated.

7. Keep Cameras and Sensors Well-Maintained

- **Clear Obstructions:** Regularly check and clear any obstructions from cameras and sensors, such as dirt, snow, or foliage, to maintain clear views and accurate detection.

- **Adjust for Seasonal Changes:** Adjust outdoor cameras and motion sensors as necessary to account for changes in light and environment, such as foliage growth or snowfall.

8. Monitor and Review Activity Logs

- **Activity Logs:** Frequently review activity logs and video footage to monitor for any unusual or suspicious activity. This can help you spot potential security breaches early.

- **Alert Customization:** Customize alert settings to receive notifications for specific activities, such as doors opening or motion detected in restricted areas.

9. Educate Family Members and Guests

- **System Usage:** Ensure all family members and frequent guests understand how to use the system, including arming/disarming procedures and responding to alarms.

- **Emergency Procedures:** Establish and regularly review emergency procedures, such as what to do if an alarm sounds or if there's an emergency situation at home.

10. Be Cautious with Smart Home Integrations

- **Device Security:** When integrating other smart home devices, ensure they are from reputable manufacturers and have robust security features.

- **Regular Updates:** Keep all integrated devices updated to the latest firmware to protect against vulnerabilities.

8

. Additional Features and Services

The Guardian Protection home security system offers several advanced features and services that go beyond basic security, providing enhanced protection and convenience. Here's a closer look at these features and how they can benefit you.

Professional Monitoring

- **24/7 Monitoring:** Guardian Protection provides round-the-clock monitoring services to respond to alarms and alerts. Their team of professionals can quickly assess situations and dispatch emergency services if needed.

- **Response Time:** Professional monitoring ensures a swift response to emergencies, reducing the time it takes to get help in critical situations.

Guardian Protection Monitoring for Business

Guardian Protection Monitoring for businesses typically refers to a comprehensive security and surveillance solution designed to safeguard a company's physical and digital assets. This service often involves several layers of protection and monitoring to ensure business continuity and security.

As a business owner, securing my commercial property was a top priority, and Guardian Protection's monitoring services have been a game-changer. From the moment I set up the system, I was impressed by the seamless installation and the intuitive user interface.

The professional monitoring service is top-notch. The 24/7 monitoring ensures that any security breach or emergency is addressed immediately, giving me peace of mind even when I'm away from the office. The response time is quick and efficient-whenever the system detects any unusual activity, the response team is on it right away, contacting me and dispatching emergency services if necessary.

The integration with smart home devices has been incredibly useful. I can control the security system remotely through the mobile app, allowing me to manage alarms, view live camera feeds, and receive instant alerts about any suspicious activity. The video surveillance quality is excellent, and the cloud storage feature provides easy access to recorded footage, which is priceless for reviewing any incidents.

Overall, Guardian Protection has exceeded my expectations. Their monitoring service has not only enhanced the security of my business but also provided a level of reliability and professionalism that's hard to beat. I highly recommend Guardian Protection to any business owner looking for a robust and dependable security solution.

Here's a breakdown of a few details:

- o **Surveillance Cameras**: Installation of CCTV cameras around key areas of the business premises to monitor and record activities.

- o **Alarm Systems**: Implementation of alarm systems for detecting unauthorized access or breaches.

- o **Access Control**: Use of electronic access systems to manage who can enter different areas of the business.

- **Network Monitoring**: Continuous monitoring of the company's network for unusual activity or potential threats.

- **Firewall Protection**: Deployment of firewalls to prevent unauthorized access to the company's digital infrastructure.

- **Intrusion Detection Systems (IDS)**: Tools to identify and respond to potential security breaches or cyberattacks.

- **Backup Solutions**: Regular backups of critical data to prevent loss due to system failures or attacks.

- **Encryption**: Protecting sensitive information through encryption to safeguard against data breaches.

- **Real-Time Alerts**: Immediate notifications in the event of a security breach or other incidents.

- **Response Plans**: Pre-established procedures for responding to different types of security incidents, including both physical and cyber threats.

- **Regulatory Compliance**: Ensuring that the business meets industry regulations and standards for security.

- **Regular Reports**: Providing detailed reports on security status, incidents, and compliance.

- **Security Assessments**: Regular assessments to identify potential vulnerabilities and improve security measures.

- **Employee Training**: Educating staff on security best practices and how to respond to potential threats.

Video Surveillance and Cloud Storage

- **Live Streaming:** Access live video feeds from your cameras anytime, anywhere, through the mobile app or control panel. This allows you to monitor your property in real time.

- **Cloud Storage:** Many systems offer cloud storage for recorded footage, allowing you to review past events and keep video records for a specified duration. This feature is crucial for investigating incidents or maintaining evidence.

Smart Home Integration

- **Home Automation:** Integrate with smart home devices like lights, thermostats, and locks for enhanced automation and control. For example, you can set up routines where lights turn on when motion is detected or adjust the thermostat when the system is armed.

AUTOMATION

AUTOMATION

Indoor Smart Plug **Outdoor Smart Plug**

- **Voice Control:** Use voice assistants like Amazon Alexa or Google Assistant to control your security system with simple voice commands. This provides a convenient way to manage your system hands-free.

AUTOMATION

Smart Garage Door Opener

Environmental Monitoring

- **Smoke and Carbon Monoxide Detectors:** Some systems include or integrate with environmental sensors that detect smoke, carbon monoxide, or natural gas leaks.

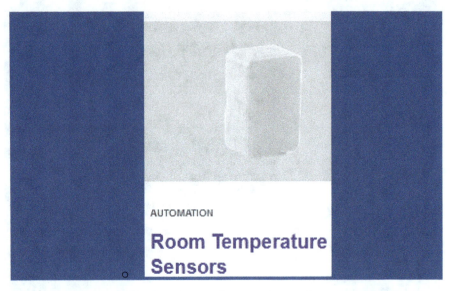

AUTOMATION

Room Temperature Sensors

- These sensors provide early warnings of potential hazards.

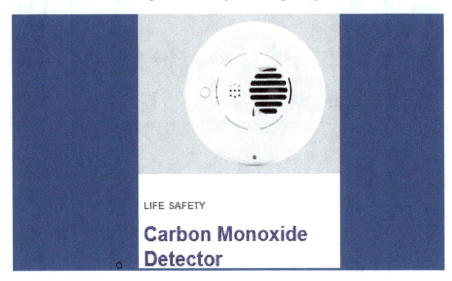

LIFE SAFETY

Carbon Monoxide Detector

- **Flood Sensors:** Install flood sensors in areas prone to water damage, such as basements or nearby appliances. These sensors alert you to potential leaks or flooding, helping to prevent significant damage.

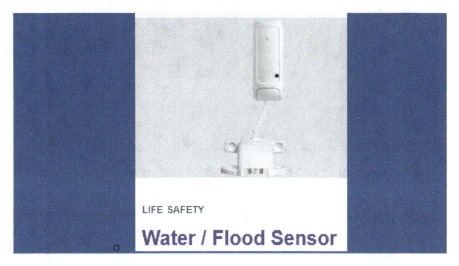

LIFE SAFETY

Water / Flood Sensor

Medical Alert Systems

- **Emergency Buttons:** For households with individuals who may need medical assistance, some systems offer emergency medical alert buttons that can quickly notify emergency services or designated contacts.

Medical alert pendant for emergencies

Medical emergencies can occur anywhere in the home. Holding a pendant within reach can assist you to quickly call for emergency help and may aid save the life of a loved one. Its medical pendant can be attached around the neck or alongside a key chain - as more convenient for a user.

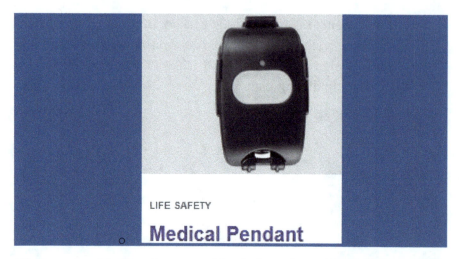

LIFE SAFETY

Medical Pendant

The press and hold pattern provides help at the push of a button. This special press-and-hold design is to reduce the chance of accidental alarms triggered by bumps or nudges.

- **Fall Detection:** Advanced systems may include fall detection technology, automatically sending alerts if a fall is detected, which is particularly useful for elderly family members.

Remote Access and Control

- **Mobile App Features:** The mobile app allows you to control your system remotely, view live video, and receive notifications. This is particularly useful for managing your security while away from home.

- **Remote Adjustments:** Make adjustments to system settings, such as changing security modes or updating notification preferences, from anywhere using your smartphone or tablet.

Home Security Cameras

- **Indoor and Outdoor Cameras:** Guardian Protection offers a range of camera options for both indoor and outdoor use.

Features such as night vision, high-definition video, and motion detection enhance surveillance capabilities.

- **Two-Way Audio:** Some cameras include two-way audio, allowing you to communicate with people on the other side of the camera. This is useful for interacting with delivery personnel or family members.

Customizable Alerts and Notifications

- **Personalized Alerts:** Customize alerts to receive notifications for specific events, such as door openings, motion detection in certain areas, or system tampering.

- **Notification Preferences:** Set preferences for how and when you receive notifications, including via text message, email, or push notifications.

- **Local Contacts:** You can program local contacts into the system who can be notified of emergencies or system status changes, providing an additional layer of security.

Customer Support and Service Plans

- **24/7 Customer Support:** Access customer support for assistance with system issues, troubleshooting, or questions about features.

- **Service Plans:** Explore various service plans offered by Guardian Protection, including maintenance packages and extended warranties, to ensure ongoing support and system reliability.

By leveraging these features and services, you can enhance the functionality and effectiveness of your Guardian Protection home security system, making it a more comprehensive solution for safeguarding your home and family.

9

Home Security Packages

Bachelor(ette) Pad

The Bachelor(ette) Pad package includes

- 24/7 Professional monitoring
- Mobile control
- Fire and burglar protection
- Guardian IQ Panel
- 3 Door / window sensors
- Motion detector
- Smoke detector
- Video doorbell pro

The Bachelor(ette) home security package is tailored for young professionals transitioning into their first home. This package provides peace of mind for those living independently by ensuring a high level of security.

Touchscreen and go: Guardian's IQ touchscreen panel allows you to touch and swipe your way to a save and smarter home. It looks and feels like a tablet, so the learning curve is less precipitous.

Package delivery notifications: watch over all your next-day deliveries from your smartphone. Because video doorbells aren't just for guarding your doorway, your expensive buying need protection, too. Know who's at your door before you throw it open- on your IQ panel.

One app: Control your home security from one easy-to-use app that you can access at home or anywhere around the world.

You don't have to be home to respond to a smoke alarm. They'll jump into action for you.

Target Audience:

- Young Professionals: Designed for individuals moving into their starter homes, whether it's their first apartment or a small house.
- Parents of Young Adults: Ideal for parents looking to provide extra security for their children leaving home for the first time.

Benefits:

- Enhanced Security: The package includes a smart security system equipped with PowerG wireless intrusion technology, which offers reliable and robust protection against intrusions.
- Ease of Use: The smart technology allows for easy monitoring and control, making it suitable for individuals who may not have extensive experience with home security systems.
- Peace of Mind: Provides confidence to young professionals living solo and reassurance for parents that their children are protected.

Ideal Scenarios:

- First-Time Homeowners: Young professionals moving into their own space for the first time can benefit from the security and convenience of a smart system.
- Parents Gifting Security: As a thoughtful gift, parents can provide their children with more than just household

essentials; they can offer the safety and security of a reliable home security system.

The Burglar Buster

The Burglar Buster package includes

- 24/7 professional monitoring
- Smart video surveillance
- Advanced encryption
- Layered protection
- Free Professional Installation
- IQ4 Control Panel
- 4 Door/Window Contacts
- 1 Smoke/Heat Detector
- 1 Motion Sensor
- 1 Smart Door Lock
- 1 Outdoor Camera
- 1 Video Doorbell

The Burglar Buster package is a comprehensive home security solution designed to address the heightened concerns of homeowners in areas with reported break-ins. This package ensures extensive coverage and advanced features to protect your property effectively.

Features- PowerG Wireless Intrusion Technology: This state-of-the-art wireless solution provides long-range capabilities, strong encryption, and reliability, ensuring secure communication between devices and the central system.

.Benefits:

Proactive Security: The Burglar Buster package allows you to detect and respond to threats before they escalate, providing peace of mind that your home is always under vigilant watch.

Complete Property Coverage: With both indoor and outdoor surveillance, you can monitor every corner of your property, ensuring comprehensive protection.

Ease of Use: The smart features and integration with mobile devices make it easy to manage and monitor your home security system from anywhere.

Ideal Scenarios:

Areas with High Crime Rates: Homeowners in neighbourhoods with frequent break-ins can significantly benefit from the enhanced security features of the Burglar Buster package.

Concerned Homeowners: For those who prioritize the safety of their property and loved ones, this package offers robust and reliable protection.

The Family First

The Family First package includes

- 24/7 Professional monitoring
- Guardian IQ Panel
- Door / window sensors (5)
- Motion detector
- Smoke & heat detector
- Carbon monoxide detector
- Video doorbell
- Smart door lock
- Indoor camera

- Outdoor camera

The Family First package is a holistic home security solution tailored for families, offering robust protection and peace of mind. It addresses not only the conventional threats like intrusions but also includes safety measures for everyday concerns, making it ideal for parents who wish to monitor and protect their loved ones, no matter their age.

Comprehensive Safety Measures:

Monitored Burglary Alarms: Protects your home from unauthorized entries, alerting you and the authorities in case of a break-in.

Smoke, Heat, and CO Alarms: Provides early warnings for fire, high temperatures, and carbon monoxide leaks, ensuring your family's safety from these hazards.

Advanced Monitoring with Smart PowerG Sensors.- also monitor specific areas or items, such as liquor cabinets or medicine drawers, to prevent unauthorized access. Receive immediate alerts on your smartphone or other connected devices.

Family-Focused Features through Remote Monitoring, Allows parents to keep an eye on their children and home, even when they are not physically present, ensuring that everything is secure. Easy-to-use controls and monitoring features make it simple for all family members to interact with the system.

Benefits:

Peace of Mind: Whether your children are young or grown, the Family First package ensures that you can always be aware of their safety and well-being.

Comprehensive Coverage: The integration of burglary, smoke, heat, and CO alarms with smart sensors provides an all-encompassing safety net for your home.

Preventive Measures: Beyond intrusion protection, the smart sensors help prevent accidents or unauthorized access to off-limits areas, adding an extra layer of security.

Ideal Scenarios:

- Families with Young Children: Parents can monitor their children's activities and ensure they stay away from dangerous areas or items.
- Families with Teenagers or Adult Children: Even when kids are older, parents can stay informed about their safety and prevent access to restricted items.
- Care for Elderly Family Members: The system can also be used to monitor elderly family members, ensuring they are safe and responding quickly to any emergencies

Pet Parent

The Pet Parent package includes

- 24/7 professional monitoring
- Video and photo capabilities
- Comfort control
- Guardian IQ panel
- Door / window sensors (3)
- Motion detector
- Smoke & heat detectors (2)
- Carbon monoxide detector
- Smart door lock
- Smart automated light modules

- Smart thermostat
- Indoor camera
- Room temperature sensor

Maybe your puppy only eat organic things or that your cat call the shots. Maybe you just want to know what your pet does all day when you're not home- check up on your best friend, make sure they're getting some daily activity, and assist keep them safe with Pet Parent package.

Help protect them from fire: With monitored smoke detectors, they can alert you and their monitoring center if abnormal levels of heat and smoke are detected. It can also send a signal to your Guardian smart thermostat- telling it to shut the air off so it doesn't push smoke throughout your home.

Dog Walker Access: Maybe you are thinking of hiring a dog walker to get your puppy some exercise while you're occupied or away. Or to provide easy and secure access to your home with a personalized smart door lock code, think of this package.

Additional Benefits

- Set up alerts synced with your smart door lock, so you'll discern if the pet sitter was a no-show.
- Keep parts of your home off limits to your pets and set up alerts to let you discern if they're somewhere they shouldn't be.
- Two-way audio: With two-way audio, you can correct your pets when you see they're up to no good.
- Pet Alert window cling: keep the pet alert sticker on a front window so that rescue personnel discern that you have pets inside.

10.

Frequently Asked Questions (FAQs)

Here are some common questions about the Guardian Protection home security system, along with their answers:

1. How do I reset my control panel?

To reset your control panel:

1. **Power Off:** Unplug the control panel from the power source.

2. **Wait:** Allow it to sit disconnected for about 30 seconds.

3. **Power On:** Plug it back in and wait for the system to reboot.

4. **Factory Reset:** For a full factory reset, refer to the user manual for specific instructions or contact customer support.

2. What should I do if my system is not responding?

If your system is unresponsive:

1. **Check Power:** Ensure the control panel is properly connected to a power source and that backup batteries are functioning.

2. **Network Connection:** Verify that your Wi-Fi or network connection is stable.

3. **Reboot:** Try restarting the system by unplugging and replugging the power.

4. **Support:** If the issue persists, contact customer support for assistance.

3. How can I add or remove user codes?

To add or remove user codes:

1. **Access Settings:** Go to the user management section on your control panel or mobile app.

2. **Add Code:** Enter a new user code and assign it to a user.

3. **Remove Code:** Select the user code you want to remove and follow the instructions to delete it.

4. **Save Changes:** Ensure you save any changes to update the system.

4. How do I change the battery in my sensors?

To change the battery:

1. **Open Sensor:** Carefully open the sensor's casing, usually by pressing or sliding a latch.

2. **Replace Battery:** Remove the old battery and insert a new one, following the polarity markings.

3. **Close Sensor:** Securely close the sensor casing and ensure it is properly reattached.

5. How can I view recorded footage from my cameras?

To view recorded footage:

1. **Access App or Control Panel:** Open the mobile app or control panel.

2. **Select Cameras:** Navigate to the camera section.

3. **View Recordings:** Access the recorded footage through the cloud storage or SD card, depending on your system's setup.

6. What should I do if I receive a false alarm?

If you receive a false alarm:

1. **Verify Trigger:** Check the system to identify what triggered the alarm, such as a sensor or camera.

2. **Adjust Sensitivity:** Review and adjust the sensitivity settings of your sensors or cameras to prevent future false alarms.

3. **Contact Support:** If false alarms continue, contact customer support for further assistance.

7. Can I integrate my system with other smart home devices?

Yes, Guardian Protection systems often integrate with various smart home devices. To do this:

1. **Check Compatibility:** Ensure your smart home devices are compatible with your security system.

2. **Follow Integration Instructions:** Use the mobile app or control panel to add and configure smart home devices according to the provided instructions.

8. How do I update the software or firmware?

To update software or firmware:

1. **Check for Updates:** The control panel or mobile app will usually notify you of available updates.

2. **Follow Prompts:** Follow the on-screen prompts to download and install updates.

3. **Restart System:** After the update, restart your system if required.

9. What should I do if my cameras are not recording?

If cameras are not recording:

1. **Check Power and Connection:** Ensure the cameras are powered and properly connected to the network.

2. **Verify Storage:** Confirm that the cloud storage or SD card has enough space and is functioning correctly.

3. **Restart Cameras:** Reboot the cameras and check if the recording resumes.

4. **Contact Support:** For ongoing issues, reach out to customer support.

10. How do I contact customer support?

To contact customer support:

1. **Phone or Email:** Use the contact information provided in your user manual or on the Guardian Protection website.

2. **Online Portal:** Many systems have an online support portal where you can submit inquiries or request assistance.

11.

Warranty and Support

Understanding the warranty and support options for your Guardian Protection home security system is very good for ensuring long-term reliability and resolving any issues that may arise.

Warranty Coverage

1. **Standard Warranty:**

    o **Duration:** Guardian Protection typically offers a standard warranty that covers parts and labour for a specified period, often 1 to 3 years, depending on the product and service plan.

    o **Coverage:** The warranty generally covers defects in materials and workmanship. This includes repairs or replacements of faulty components, such as control panels, sensors, and cameras.

2. **Extended Warranty:**

    o **Options:** Extended warranty plans may be available for purchase, extending coverage beyond the standard period. These plans might offer additional benefits, such as extended repair or replacement coverage and priority service.

- o **Details:** Check with Guardian Protection or your authorized dealer for details on available extended warranty plans and what they include.

3. **Exclusions:**

- o **User Damage:** The warranty typically does not cover damage resulting from misuse, accidents, or unauthorized modifications.

- o **Consumables:** Items such as batteries, which have a limited lifespan, may not be covered under the warranty.

Support Services

1. **Customer Support:**

- o **Contact Methods:** You can reach customer support through various channels, including phone, email, and online chat. The contact information is usually provided in the user manual or on the Guardian Protection website.

- o **Availability:** Support is typically available during business hours, but some services may offer 24/7 support for urgent issues or emergencies.

2. **Technical Support:**

- o **Assistance:** Technical support can help with system setup, troubleshooting, and configuration issues. They can guide you through common problems and provide solutions.

- o **Remote Support:** In many cases, support representatives can remotely access your system to diagnose and resolve issues.

3. **Service and Repairs:**

   - o **Authorized Technicians:** Repairs are often performed by authorized technicians who are trained to handle Guardian Protection systems. They can service or replace components as needed.

   - o **Service Requests:** To request service or repairs, contact customer support to schedule an appointment. They will guide you through the process and provide instructions on how to prepare for the technician's visit.

4. **Online Resources:**

   - o **FAQs and Manuals:** The Guardian Protection website often provides a comprehensive FAQ section and user manuals that can help you troubleshoot issues and understand system features.

   - o **Video Tutorials:** Some systems offer video tutorials or online guides for setup, maintenance, and troubleshooting.

5. **Upgrades and Add-Ons:**

   - o **New Features:** You may be able to upgrade your system or add new features, such as additional cameras or smart home integrations. Contact customer support or your authorized dealer to explore available options and pricing.

Warranty and Support Tips

1. **Keep Documentation:** Retain your purchase receipt, warranty registration, and any service records. This documentation will be helpful if you need to claim warranty coverage or request support.

2. **Read Warranty Terms:** Familiarize yourself with the terms and conditions of your warranty to understand what is covered and any limitations or exclusions.

3. **Regular Maintenance:** Perform regular maintenance and follow best practices to prevent issues and ensure your system remains under warranty.

12.

Safety Information and Legal Notices

When using the Guardian Protection home security system, it is vital to follow safety guidelines and be aware of legal notices to ensure safe operation and compliance with regulations. Here's a comprehensive overview of the safety and legal considerations associated with your system.

Safety Information

1. **Installation Safety:**

   o **Professional Installation:** If recommended, use professional installation services to ensure the system is set up correctly and safely. Incorrect installation can affect system performance and safety.

   o **Electrical Safety:** Ensure that all electrical connections are properly installed and avoid overloading power outlets.

2. **Handling and Maintenance:**

   o **Avoid Tampering:** Do not tamper with or modify the system components. Unauthorized modifications can void the warranty and compromise system functionality.

- **Proper Cleaning:** Clean components, such as sensors and cameras, with appropriate methods (e.g., using a soft cloth) to avoid damage.

3. **Emergency Procedures:**

   - **Testing Alarms:** Regularly test alarms and sensors to ensure they are functioning correctly. Follow instructions in the user manual for safe testing procedures.

   - **Emergency Response:** Familiarize yourself with emergency procedures and ensure all household members know how to respond to alarms and alerts.

4. **Battery Safety:**

   - **Battery Replacement:** Use only recommended battery types and replace them as needed. Dispose of old batteries according to local regulations to prevent environmental harm.

   - **Leakage and Damage:** Avoid exposure to extreme temperatures and moisture, which can damage batteries and affect system performance.

5. **Children and Pets:**

   - **System Placement:** Place sensors and cameras out of reach of children and pets to prevent accidental interference or damage.

   - **Training:** Educate household members, including children, about the proper use of the security system and the importance of not tampering with it.

Legal Notices

1. **Privacy and Data Protection:**

   o **Data Collection:** Guardian Protection may collect personal information and data as part of system operation and monitoring. Review the privacy policy to understand how your data is collected, used, and protected.

   o **Consent:** By using the system, you consent to the collection and use of your data as outlined in the privacy policy. Ensure you are comfortable with the terms before installation.

2. **Compliance with Regulations:**

   o **Local Laws:** Ensure your use of the security system complies with local regulations and ordinances regarding surveillance and alarm systems. Some jurisdictions may have specific requirements or restrictions.

   o **Notification Requirements:** Some areas may require you to notify local authorities or obtain permits for installing security systems with surveillance capabilities.

3. **System Limitations:**

   o **Not a Substitute for Professional Monitoring:** While the Guardian Protection system enhances home security, it is not a substitute for professional monitoring and emergency services. The system may have limitations, such as potential delays in response or false alarms.

- o **Liability:** Guardian Protection is not liable for any damages or losses resulting from system failure, misuse, or external factors that affect the system's performance.

4. **Warranty Terms:**

   - o **Coverage and Exclusions:** Review the warranty terms and conditions to understand what is covered and any exclusions. Compliance with the warranty terms is necessary to maintain coverage and ensure valid claims.

5. **End-User License Agreement (EULA):**

   - o **Software Usage:** By using the Guardian Protection system, you agree to the End-User License Agreement (EULA) associated with any software or mobile applications. Review the EULA to understand your rights and obligations regarding software use.

6. **Intellectual Property:**

   - o **Copyright and Trademarks:** All intellectual property rights related to the Guardian Protection system, including trademarks, copyrights, and patents, are owned by Guardian Protection or its licensors. Unauthorized use of these intellectual properties is prohibited.

Contact Information for Legal Inquiries

- **Customer Support:** For any legal inquiries or concerns regarding the system's operation, warranty, or compliance, contact Guardian Protection's customer support team for assistance and guidance.

By adhering to these safety guidelines and understanding the legal notices, you can ensure the safe and compliant use of your Guardian Protection home security system.

ISBN 9798334923515